Inspired

by the Craitor

A drop of the hard stuff

By

Desmond Lynch

*Jackie
Enjoy the Read
Dessie Lynch*

Copyright © Desmond Lynch 2024
This book is sold subject to the condition that it shall not, by way of trade or otherwise, be lent, resold, hired out, or otherwise circulated without the publisher's prior consent in any form of binding or cover other than that in which it is published and without a similar condition including this condition being imposed on the subsequent publisher.
The moral right of Desmond Lynch has been asserted.

For Tish,

Thank you for all the wonderful years we've had together.

CONTENTS

A Drop of the Craitor 1
A Cry for Peace and Justice 3
Grandad's Reminiscings 5
A Moment to Meander 7
A Notion for a Potion 8
A Notorious Feat 10
All Walks of Life 12
Beautiful Gweedore 14
Contentment 16
Don't Ever Wish Your Life Away 18
Don't Hurry Tomorrow 20
Éirinn Go Brách 22
Forever Our Matriarch 23
Grandchildren 24
Habits Have No Pockets 26
Hair Today and Gone Tomorrow 28
I Can Almost Hear A Passing Cloud 30
I Once Loved and Shared a Kiss 32
I Pray 34
I Said Goodnight 35
I Wish I Could Hibernate 37
I'll Raise My Glass 39
In Search of Utopia 41
Life's Journey (The Class of '61) 43
My Royal County Meath 45
No One Can Hear A Silent Cry 47
Nonsense Thinking 49
Old Samuel 51
Precious Stones 53
Prolong I'll Try 55

Quest for Energy	57
Regret Not Time	59
Regret	61
Strut Your Stuff	62
Thank You for Saying I Do	63
The "Benefits" of Age	65
The Candlestick Days	67
The Croppy Grave	69
The Mammy's Brown Bread	71
The Proper Antidote	73
The Road to No Return	74
Through Purple Haze	76
To Have a Magic Wand	78
Trade Not Time for Dreams	80
We Too Were Once Oppressed	82
What's the Harm	84
Who is Your Mum?	85
With Best Intentions	86
You Didn't Hear Me	88
You Never Forget to Pray	90
A Monumental Bender	92
A Smiling Face A Crying Heart	94
A Visit In Peace	95
Convulsive Verse by an Ordinary Person	97
Cursed Emigration	99
Don't Ask Me To Do The Dishes	101
Echoes From Long Ago	103
Ninety Seconds to Midnight	105
Our Destiny	107
Samuel They Can Kiss My Ass	109
Simply For Tish	111
Splendid Conditions	112
Spring	113
The Howling Winds	115
Two Hearts Of Gold	117

What They Call Graceful... 118
Whittling Away The Hours 120
Who Can Say 122
Who Cares... 124

A Drop of the Craitor

As we grow older and on in the years
And in our heads are new found fears
When old friends leave and not seen thereafter
It's time to have a drop of the craitor

When we find it difficult to get out of bed
And our two legs weigh like lead
But between we still have a urinater
Sure it's safe enough to have a drop of the craitor

When we can't bend down to tie our laces
And are jaded tired after a few paces
It will never be sooner but always later
Take your time and have a drop of the craitor

When we are trying to button up our shirt
And we feel our fingers and thumbs hurt
Before they become any frailer
Make sure to have a drop of the craitor

When we can't kneel down to say a prayer
And we are left standing up to curse and swear
When we begin to sound like an orator
It's past time to have a drop of the craitor

When our hand can no more make a fist
And we no longer can pucker our lips to be kissed
Make sure they are in position to cater
For our daily drop of the craitor.

A Cry for Peace and Justice

Evil warlords wicked men
Sheath your sword and pick up your pen
Write not history with man's blood
But document it in ink instead

Heinous old men angry and decrepit
Sending young soldiers bold and intrepid
In search of glory on a battlefield
But only the stench of death does it yield

Wealth is so wrongly spent and squandered
Gratifying the lust of you mongered
If diverted to feed just one hungry soul
'Twould be a triumphant and worthy goal

Lust and greed has consumed mankind
Dignity and generosity is harder to find
No more one for all and all for one
The days of chivalry are long gone

If only peacemakers were at the helm
There'd be more equality on our orbital realm
No waste of food no more hunger
Peace on Earth would grow much stronger

We have a planet that can endure,
All our ails and provide a cure.
We just need to obliterate,
The men of evil who desecrate.

Grandad's Reminiscings

I brought you up as best I could
But I didn't do it as I should
I lived too hard and didn't think
And life has passed in just a blink

Thank God you had a very good mum
She kept your life from been so glum
Working fifty two seven, I was seldom there
And as long as I live I can never repair

Not being there when you were growing up
I'm sitting here thinking and drinking a sup
Wondering why I was such a fool
Not being there for your days in school

I look back and feel a little sad
It wasn't that I was a bad old dad
There was always a bill to be paid
And money wasn't easily made

We done our best to make you happy
But it was your mum who always changed your nappy
She was the one who was always there
It was your mum who gave you all the care

But I am proud to see the way you turned out
And not following me on the same old route
Enjoying your children while they are young
Keeping your patience and holding your tongue

I'm a grandad now and so very glad
To be given a second chance to be a dad
I love my grandchildren with all my heart
As I have loved you from the very start.

A Moment to Meander

Between my selfish and giving self I'm torn
My mind is drained and body worn
No one is to blame, it's no one's fault
Life's journey is slowly coming to a halt

If I could get one moment to meander
Down the boreens I once did wander
And embellish my mind and soul with memoirs
When I first saw the plough in the stars

To lose myself in the abyss of time
Is a fantasy journey in my rhyme?
When gravity can't hold me down
And I'm sailing the heavens in a silver gown

My hallucination has come to an end
And back to Earth I descend
But those glimpses from the past I was shown
Will give me the strength to carry on.

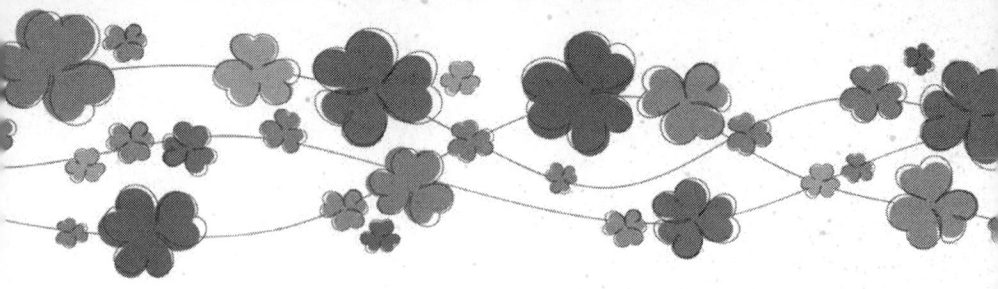

A Notion for a Potion

I have in my head this notion
If I could concoct a magic potion
To heal the world of all its ills
And free us all from taking pills

Ingredients that are simple and pure
That would provide us with a miraculous cure
For every ailment under the sun
Pardon the expression and excuse the pun

A concoction to cheer us up when sad
And keep us sane when going mad
To give us a boost when we feel like dying
Make us laugh when we are crying

A compound to enlighten when feeling stupid
Improve our aim when playing cupid
To steer us from our erring ways
And free us from that labyrinthine maze

A tonic to take the cobwebs from our heart
And vanish every pimple, spot, and wart
A lubrication to oil our vocal cords
To sing our songs with melodious words

A brew that enhances inebriation
Provides a feeling of exhilaration
Sure I'll look no further than the poteen still
Won't the Mountain Dew just fit the bill.

A Notorious Feat

Life can be callous and sometimes cruel
Not perfected and no crown jewel
It can be sad and lonely or full of joy
It can ego boost or soul destroy

Having lived through most emotions
Calm seas and stormy oceans
Surviving pandemics and depressions
Recovered from some mighty sessions

Everyone needs to go to town
Give it a lash and let their hair down
Can't always be a holy and pious Joe
Got to let that adrenaline flow

Life can be a roller coaster or damp squib
Are we buoyant or do we moan and crib
Song and dance brings out the best
An Irish wake puts a soul to rest

Been on quite a few benders
When there was only two biological genders
Nothing intricated or complicated
Smart arses then were not tolerated

One shot is all we get
Live it good, without regret
A journey short so make it sweet
A hundred years would be a notorious feat.

All Walks of Life

I walked through life in all directions
Down byways and through intersections
I rambled down the auld boreen
More times than umpteen

I roamed the hills and the valley below
And listened to the river waters flow
On heady days I'd be a dreamer
Never yearning for pastures greener

I walked on warm sandy beaches
And lazed in their shady niches
I waded in the water by the seashore
Hearing the lapping waves roar

I walked on many a tightrope
With little manoeuvre and not much scope
I will never walk on red hot coals
Be too much like hell, with the burning "soles"

Done my fair share of walking on air
Head held high and wind in my hair
I walked with the sun beaming down on my face
I knew from then this was my place

I'm not ready to walk into the sunset
There's more to do in this life yet
With my mind at peace and soul in His hand
My heart still belongs to dear old Ireland.

Beautiful Gweedore

Oh beautiful, beautiful Gweedore
Nestling on the Atlantic shore
Your beauty and charm is so bewitching
To my soul you are so enriching

Your way of life your generous ways
Reminds me of my childhood days
With no turned keys in your front doors
So much trust in friends and neighbours

Your winding roads, your rising hills
With wanderlust my heart fills
To be a wee bird on a wing
Over your hilltops I would sing

The valleys you have down below
To your scenery, I take a bow
I have walked upon your golden strands
With my love holding hands

The purple heather on your boglands
Landscaped only by natures hands
Your Mount Errigal reaching ever so high
Parting the clouds and kissing the sky

The beautiful islands off your shore
Your Atlantic sunset I do adore
The silvery moon over the ocean
It's the mirror image in gentle motion

Sadly now I have to say goodbye
But thank you for this moment of joy
I promise someday I will return
Before it's time for me to adjourn.

Contentment

I was born and raised in the middle of nowhere
With your cities and towns you cannot compare
Living in the countryside of County Meath
Fresher air you will not breathe

The dawn of day is a great time to stroll
It tunes your brain for your daily roll
Breathing in such pure fresh air
How could your mind ever despair?

Hawkinstown is where I fondly dwell
It's much nearer to heaven than to hell
I love it so much I want to live forever
An impossible feat, beyond my endeavour

Down the road is the Bridge of Balgeeth
Its rippling waters flowing beneath
Just to stand here is such a treasure
It's serenity you cannot measure

I walk my dogs across the fields
It's amazing what this saunter yields
My body and soul feels so free
I'm so elated I could hug a tree

As long as I'm alive I'll enjoy this place
I'm the happiest person in the human race
I could not live in any city or town
My brow would be furrowed with a frown

When I die I would like my spirit to roam
Around these hills I call my home
Hawkinstown, to me is hallowed ground
A more tranquil place will not be found.

Don't Ever Wish Your Life Away

It's crazy the way we think
That we'd sacrifice a day in a blink
For just tomorrow to be here
We'd wish for today to disappear

Boredom is the primary cause
Unable to sit still and pause
Idle hands create mischievous minds
Wishing time away are the signs

The stress of life we try to elude
Fantasizing to enhance our mood
Dreaming and craving for carefree play
Sure we are only wishing our life away

To failures we have succumbed
Feeling paralysed and physically numbed
Yearning to recover without delay
We unwittingly wish our life away

Ambition should come with contentment
And apathy received with resentment
Live for the now and present day
Not wishing our life away

All the storms in life we rode
Without a red or yellow code
Time was the cause of our decay
Don't ever wish your life away.

Don't Hurry Tomorrow

This short life is so strange
Not long ago old age seemed out of range
Believing I would forever remain young
Notions that couldn't have been more wrong

Hindsight is a wonderful thing
The wealth of knowledge it did bring
If I knew then what I know now
All the ground I harrowed after the plough

Don't hurry the day called tomorrow
Never be looking for time to borrow
Spend only what you can afford
Never squander it by being bored

Live life good and live it true
Then fond memories you will accrue
To be able to look back without contrition
Body and soul will have no friction

Sing your song and sing it loud
Sing it alone and sing it in a crowd
Dance to the fiddle, dance to the tune
The joy of it all will keep you immune

Live life as long as you can
And calculate not its span
Live it laughing and live it loving
It will compensate all the pushing and shoving.

Éirinn Go Brách

Goddess Érin do not weep
Though heartache and sorrow runs deep
From the Hill of Uisneach we hear you cry
But cometh the hour when you can sigh

Your loyal people will answer your call
And liberate you from this corrupt Dáil
The crooked barons on your island
Will face justice and rendered silent

No more vultures feasting your bones
Or bankers calling in their exorbitant loans
Your people will be free once again
Free from despair and free from pain

There will be shelter for your homeless and destitute
And medication for the sick and mute
There'll be a helping hand for the deprived
A glorious new dawn will have arrived

Your mountains will again echo sweet melodies
And your valleys buzzing with honey bees
A new awakening will cover your land
With equality and justice clenched in your hand.

Forever Our Matriarch

(A Tribute to Ciss)

You took the reins and showed us how
To harrow the sod after we plough
Rising earlier than the morning lark
You truly are our matriarch

You set example by demonstration
Tirelessly toiling without cessation
From dawn of day until after dark
You truly are our matriarch

Always a smile and genteel manner
You proudly carried the "for mothers" banner
In your lifetime you made your mark
You truly are our matriarch

You travelled life's journey as God wished
Your mission now is fully accomplished
God has raised you way above the lark
You'll be forever our matriarch.

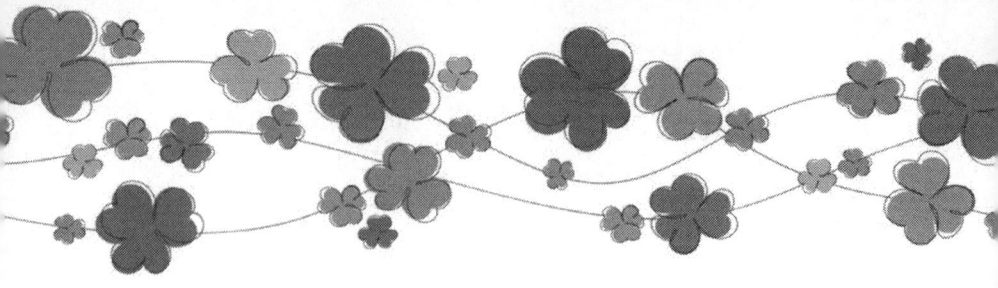

Grandchildren

Grandkids, where would we be without you
Treasures like you are far too few
I'm glad you came along my way
Even though I had no say

You are each so different and complete
I love you all from your very first bleat
You are each your own unique self
Varying as much as china and delph

Equality is a factor of my affection
If that's wrong, I stand for correction
I love a smile and a cheeky grin
I love your laughter and noisy din

So precious are your hugs and cuddles
And the way you jump in water puddles
The jam you get all over your little face
Gives those hugs and kisses a sweeter taste

You keep us grandparents young at heart
And our minds and bodies on high alert
Your mischievous ways can lead to danger
We would need to be a ninja turtle ranger

I never mind been asked to babysit
But don't ask me to change a nappy full of s**t
I can babysit you for quite awhile
But giving you back brings on a smile

If I live to be a ripe old age
I'd like to be your personal sage
Telling you stories from my yesteryear
And when I'm gone you'd hold them dear.

Habits Have No Pockets

What's the ethos of a billionaire
Is there a gene or something more rare
That elevates him above his fellowman
Can he see further than his gold mining pan

The time will come to us all
When the Grimreaper makes his call
Does he think with all his wealth
He can offer a bribe and cheat his death

Leaving this world whether angelic or wicked
There's no fee for that one way ticket
And the habit has no secret pockets
Rendering legal tender to redundant dockets

We came onto this Earth without any clothing
So leave with dignity, not contemptuous loathing
Materialism has no fervent use
Excessive hoarding is wanton abuse

If only charity overtook greed
All the living souls that would be freed
From poverty, hunger and malnutrition
Only then will righteousness come to fruition

The Native American only served his need
No random waste and hollow greed
Mother Earth he said would provide
Until "civilisation" cast that aside

Greed is one of the seven deadly sins
To which unending lust vigorously clings
To give and to serve is much more rewarding
Than all of the stockpiling and baneful hoarding.

Hair Today and Gone Tomorrow

There's a few things to be said about hair
If it's not on your head then your crown is bare
The brush and comb don't have anything to groom
And as for the lice and nits, it's a place of doom

Baldness is the curse of mankind
Remedies and antidotes are impossible to find
Once they thought they had the cure
A simple ingredient called hen manure

It was thought poultry farmers shaved more frequent
Conclusions were jumped upon it was the hens excrement
It wasn't long before this shite was in a jar
And upon baldness they declared a war

That craze fizzled out fairly swift
There wasn't a woman a man could shift
Aftershaves and lotions couldn't kill the smell
Regrowing hair was just a living hell

The pattern of its growth is very finical
As we age it becomes more and more cynical
Growing profusely from our ears, nose, and anus
Places that are the least most famous

Hair today and gone tomorrow
Times of joy and times of sorrow
A topic of interest to say the least
It's either a famine or glorious feast.

I Can Almost Hear A Passing Cloud

Lying awake when sleep has forsaken,
All my anxieties and worries awaken.
Eyes wide open, my mind unloading,
As all common sense begins imploding.

Tossing and turning with weary eyes
Inhaling and exhaling laden sighs
Worrying about the most of everything
As my subconscious alarm bells ring

The silence of the night is so loud
I can almost hear a passing cloud
Casting its shadow on the moon
The dawn of day can't come too soon

I hear my heartbeat pound
Pummelling my eardrums with its sound
I hold my breath to listen
Causing a beat to go missing

I hear the chirping of a cricket
Out in the dark and dewy thicket
A vociferous sound in the still of night
I'm wishing for the morning light

Panic attacks inflict appalling fear
When no one's about and no one near
Thinking each breath will be your last
You become remorseful of your past

God, will I ever get to sleep?
Into a coma dark and deep
And sleep all my forebodings away
To waken afresh the following day.

I Once Loved and Shared a Kiss

Where's the bottle I had last night
Did I drink it all on this derelict site
I'm almost certain it wasn't empty
Could have sworn I still had plenty

Was there a thief in my midst
Stealing my whiskey while I was pissed
It's not safe sleeping in a cardboard box
There are no doors with safety locks

Intoxication helps to quell my fear
Let it be whiskey, wine, or beer
Narcotics serve to ease the pain
When sleeping rough in the cold and rain

It's not my fault I'm now living life like this
I once loved and shared a kiss
Things happen in life and things go wrong
So I ended up where I don't belong

People can be so aloof and judgemental
Unaware you are a lost soul meek and gentle
If they'd spare you a moment of their time
They would determine you committed no crime

Addiction is the scourge of mankind
Like a thief in the night comes to mind
Stealing our capacity to be in control
Injurious to our mind, body, and soul

Successive governments caused this blight
Uncaring and unrepentant of our plight
While a roof over our heads is all we sought
All we hear are the echoes of "to Hell or Connaught".

I Pray

I pray tonight passes by
Without whimper or distressing cry
That you sleep in peace and content
And nightmares are entirely absent

I pray I will hear your sighs
That no cessation will arise
I worry not about being kept awake
My concern is for your sake

I pray you will not twist and turn
But to rest you will adjourn
I'll tuck you in nice and cosy
And be rewarded by cheeks so rosy

I pray for the very next morn
To see both of us reborn
To be together for another day
For what more can I pray.

I Said Goodnight

I said goodnight while you were asleep
With a kiss on the lips for you to keep
Your pause for breath and intermittent sigh
I pray your dreams will bring you joy

I said goodnight while you tossed and turned
From delirium when your fever burned
T'was with fear that my heart was filled
Until your brow became dry and chilled

I said goodnight while you were snoring
With your every breath, I was scorning
Realising I was hearing you breathe
To this annoyance I would soon concede

I said goodnight while you were serene
You looked an angel, or maybe queen
I felt so happy you were mine
Your compassion is, so sweeter than wine

I said goodnight while asleep you smiled
Watching you smile, I silently cried
To see you in such a happy pose
I fell asleep nose to nose

I said goodnight while we have grown old
And I thank you for your heart of gold
Our vows were for better or worse
We have withstood the time and stayed the course.

I Wish I Could Hibernate

Autumn is here and winter is nigh
The swallows have flown leaving an empty sky
The leaves are changing to their seasonal colour
And the days are frequently becoming duller

The sun is lowering itself in our hemisphere
The best has gone of this present year
Storm clouds will soon be a gathering
And life becomes dormant until the spring

Days are shorter and the nights are longer
We feed the birds to stave off hunger
I envy the wildlife that can hibernate
Sleeping through winter until spring they wait

Wakening up to a cold morning frost
Leaves us no choice but to be winters host
How do we welcome weather so cold
A season that puts everything on hold

There's a burden this moment on my shoulder
The depression weights like a boulder
Carrying it until the day of solstice
When once again, I'll begin to rejoice

Knowing spring is now not far away
Back to the gardening and arousing of the clay
Nourishing and replenishing it's every need
Feeding and cultivating and preparing for new seed.

I'll Raise My Glass

Whiskey you are a friend and saviour
Though your spirit can alter my behaviour
But if we can stay friends and get along
I'll raise my glass and sing you a song

You are an inspiration to me
Giving me guidance when I can't see
Bestowing me with courage when I was scared
I'll raise my glass to the way you cared

When my heart was broken you gave me comfort
In loneliness you gave me support
I'm very thankful for your resilience
I'll raise my glass to your brilliance

You are my prescription and cureall
With more remedies than the doctor on call
For colds and flu I'll drink you hot
And I'll raise my glass from the cot

What did we do before you were distilled
With all the stress and strain that we were filled
When low and behold from the barley you were born
I'll raise my glass to that precious corn

My taste buds now do double flips
Every time you kiss my lips
To each time my palate you soak
I'll raise my glass to your barrel of oak.

In Search of Utopia

I pray for this world to be a better place
A sanctuary for all of the human race
That all conflicts and wars would cease
All weapons be decommissioned for the sake of peace

That there be no more starvation or hunger
Where malnutrition is no longer
Contented children on their mother's arm
Mothers feeling safe from all harm

To reside on a planet of plenty
With no class distinction and no gentry
No justification for excess quantity
Living in a world of balanced equality

Where respect and tolerance is exercised
And all our lives less commercialised
When apathy and greed become more balanced
Then our lives may become more enhanced

We are all entitled to peace of mind
No stress or strain of any kind
No worries about making ends meet
Knowing there'll always be a bite to eat

Yellow or red, brown, black, or white
Skin pigment declares no dominant right
We are all equal in God's eyes
Something we all have to realise.

Lifes Journey (The Class of 61)

My eyes are welling up with tears
As you take me back to those yesteryears
I thank you for this trip extraordinaire
A priceless journey without a fare

To a time so distant in my past
An expanse of age so wide and vast
Traipsing backdown this long memory lane
Learning the loss of past comrades causes pain

Your data has me overwhelmed
More than I can ever comprehend
We were only teenage boys back then
T'was when we parted we became young men

Some who later met an arduous time
Emigrating afar without cent or dime
Details of their demise that have unfurled
I shamefully feel in a different world

For I have never left my beloved country
The joys of our culture and all its bounty
There were hard times and ominous struggles
Compensated by family and loving cuddles

My heart is heavy with the thought
Of the conflict in life these men fought
And to be interred in a foreign land
With not a grain of Irish sand

I pray they have found everlasting peace
That their troubles and loneliness did cease
I pray they are at the right hand of God
Even though buried neath that foreign sod

To all of us that are left
We can't help but feel bereft
Let's all pray we have long winter years
It's the prescription for less tears.

My Royal County Meath

We have no mountain range in Co. Meath
But the beauty of our pastures you must concede
All across our plains and over to Skryne
Is a true illustration of our emerald green

The River Boyne flows through our fair land
Journeying to Mornington where it meets the strand
Perpetually flowing by night and by day
Generating peace and tranquillity on the way

The royal county once seated Ireland's high kings
Savouring the sound of a harp as a maiden sings
On the Hill of Tara where they reigned with might
Defending their realm and putting an enemy to flight

Across the valley lies the Hill of Slane
Where Patrick first lit the Paschal flame
Arrested, and brought before the royal dock
He converted the High King with a sprig of shamrock

The castle ruins that adorn our skyline
Are history's comparison to a vintage wine
Banquets entertained the noble and renowned
Humoured by a jester prancing around

Forlorn shadows they now do cast
Derelict evidence of a grandeur past
Their crumbling towers and falling arches
Slowly decaying as time marches

The historic site of Brú Na Bóinn
Or Newgrange as it's better known
This revered place, once a Neolithic crypt
Is older than the pyramids of Ancient Egypt

Navan is the capital of our domain
From where our local authorities reign
Where the rivers Boyne and Blackwater merge
Romancing since the dawn of age.

No One Can Hear A Silent Cry

Life was once a shining light
Now just flickering in the night
With no renewable energy source
The flame has almost run its course

When darkness overshadows this light
Despair becomes a haunting plight
When sanity takes a back seat
There's an assent to defeat

No one hears a silent cry
Reticence can soul destroy
Muteness will not be heard
Doesn't mean no one cared

No one can read a troubled mind
Where prosperity once wined and dined
There's so many ways to display
Everything's hunky dorey and okay

Yesterday is past tense
Today is the day of commence
Tomorrow is just maybe
We have to wait and see

Take care of your mental health
It's the most precious of all wealth
So important to retain your satire
And fulfil your life's desire.

Nonsense Thinking

I'm lost for words for the thoughts in my head
But sure words are only spoken and read
Thoughts and thinking go much deeper
With your unspoken thoughts you are still their keeper

Did you ever think about your own thoughts
Scheming and thinking devious plots
The thinking and planning for the future
Thoughts of the past you affectionally nurture

Thoughts, I'm thinking are an ambiguous puzzle
Some to share and others to muzzle
Thinking out loud can be risky and perilous
If inaccurate or anyway spurious

You know when you think about it all
Thinking is the brain's primary call.
Without thinking, its function would be meager
But thoughts in motion keep it in gear

Don't ever think your brain takes a rest
Because thinking is what it knows best
Think of the times your eyes stop blinking
Dreams and nightmares are its nightshift thinking

These are nonsense thoughts to keep you thinking
I'm thinking now of your brain cells clinking
You'll not be able to think the same again
Thinking you read this rubbish written with my pen.

Old Samuel

The pandemic came and all seemed lost
T'was Lady Luck that our paths crossed
You coming all the way from Kentucky
Me being Irish and born lucky

Where would I be without you Old Samuel
You became my survival kit and manual
Whenever I was down and in the dumps
You became my ace of trumps

You're my genie in the bottle
When performing sluggish you rev my throttle
Though you never granted me my three wishes
When you hit my palate you taste delicious

When embracing my lips endorphins flare
Leaving me in no doubt and without care
Inspiring my mind and erasing worry
Alluring me into a mode of lesser hurry

You have the shenanigans of a rapscallion
The makings of a compatible companion
We had a ball the last few years
Fulfilling appetites and chasing beers

Alas Old Samuel, time takes its toll
You a friendly spirit, me a lost soul
Mortal me whose soul from this life will sever
While you'll live on forever and ever.

Precious Stones

These stones by the side of the road
Were once a humble and modest abode
A house where people lived and people died
Where people laughed and people cried

The straw thatch roof and whitewashed walls
With two half doors always opened to calls
A lighting candle in the window frame
Inviting the night traveller to its flame

An open fire with a hob each side
Sods of turf filling an empty void
A kettle hanging from the crane
Held firmly by its crook and chain

The dresser filled with shining delph
All in order on their proper shelf
Table and chairs on the stone slabbed floor
T'was the trend from those days of yore

There was warmth from the cold of the night
In the flickering shadows of the candlelight
A place to lay down a weary head
Until dawn's light, when the darkness fled

Prayer had its place in this homestead
Each night the family rosary was said
Kneeling down with their rosary beads
They'd pray for just essential needs

Alas, the thatch has returned to the ground
But the memories are still abound
No half doors that once opened wide
Only these stones by the roadside.

Prolong I'll Try

I never dreamt I'd ever grow old
Nor the blood in my veins would run cold
That my limbs would become feeble and weak
Unthought of when I was at my peak

Never realising I reached the top
Until the fast forwarded years I tried to stop
They had gathered momentum with such speed
To the right of way I had to yield

We were always wishing our lives away
When going to school every other day
The best days of your life we were told
By a mother with a heart of gold

Did we listen? I fear not
We knew everything or so we thought
Her words of wisdom still echo in my mind
Our thoughts toward her were so unkind

We mellowed as the years have passed
Life no longer seems so vast
The remainder is less than what's gone by
I'll not complain but prolong I'll try

I have an innermost peace of mind
Meditation and prayer helped me find
So peaceful to be prepared
With the knowledge I really cared.

Quest for Energy

From the paraffin lamp to candlelight
When the power of steam was an awesome sight
Man seemed to be on the road to prosperity
With discoveries and inventions from here to eternity

To every problem he found a solution
Unaware he was causing pollution
Since he discovered coal and oil
How much damage has he done to the soil

Pollution to the water, pollution to the air
Has he damaged the ozone beyond repair?
The ice is melting on the polar caps
It won't take long till it alters our maps

We are endeavouring to turn the tide around
And put our planet on a footing more sound
It's our duty to clean up these fossil fumes
And rid our skies from the smokey plumes

Our scientists are working day and night
Doing their utmost to get things right
For too long we are leaning on the Arab crutch
Burning their oil and trapped in their clutch

Atomic energy has cast a deadly cloud
Chernobyl has warned us of the dangers unfound
When meltdown began there was no buffer
Even the unborn had to suffer

We have the means and the technology
Renewable energy is modern ontology
Convincing people it is the way to go
Is an uphill struggle and very slow

We have solar energy without a doubt
Energy until our star burns out
Our glorious sun that gives the moon light
Will give us energy day and night

For the sake of humanity this is my plea
Let's use the word we a little more than me
And help each other to a better way
Promoting a cleaner environment and less decay.

Regret Not Time

How many people have left it too late
To reconcile, and abandon their lust to hate
How many children have forsaken a parent
Not realising love is hates great deterrent

Shame on you peddlers of misery and pain
Creating rift for their own avenging bane
Their ill gotten ways beggars belief
Stealing love is the worst kind of thief

Young people who are coerced down this path
Stand firm and exert your wrath
Make it known it's not the route you desire
That it's surely the highway to your ire

Don't be influenced by such evil
Bow not to creators of destruction and upheaval
Rise above their malicious agenda
Be no part of their vengeful vendetta

Live your life and go with your gut
Life is too short to be lived in a rut
Don't be a tool for those who hate
Don't be the one who left it too late

The morning my dad passed away
God gave us time to have our last say
By his bedside we had our last chat
So at peace... when with him I sat.

Regret

Sadness and sorrow overcame us all
When a loved one got the final call
Guilt and regret struck my mind
The queries I fobbed off and declined

So many unanswered questions now
Finding those answers I know not how
I allowed them to slip away with your soul
Do you realise death, what you just stole

Ask the questions before it's too late
Do it now, don't hesitate
Endure not the anguish of the unsaid
For it's too late when the obituary is read

If I only had one more day
To say the things I wanted to say
If there was another day I could borrow
To do, what I said I'd do tomorrow.

Strut Your Stuff

When you reach the age of seventy four
And creeping closer to that exit door
If you are thinking of giving it one last fling
Just strut your stuff and do your thing

Don't let good memories run cold
Remember the past, let your thoughts unfold
Stay strong, keep young and remain alert
There's still plenty to do on this Earth

Never stop thinking anew
Don't bite off more than you can chew
You're long enough now in the tooth
To know you no longer possess your youth

Always be kind to others
Look upon them as sisters and brothers
Live every day as if it's your last
For that day is surely coming to past.

Thank You for Saying I Do

Tell me dearest, where did all those years go
Where has the time gone does anyone know
A half century has past now
Since we took our marriage vow

Happy years they were, no doubt
But we must have taken the shortest route
Seems like only yesterday
We took that trip down matrimonial way

I thank you for saying "I do"
I'm so glad I did too
Couldn't imagine my life otherwise
I love you more than I'll ever realise

You blessed me with three precious children
Our very own beloved little brethren
I can't thank you nearly enough
You were always there when times got tough

Now living our autumn years
Lets raise our glass to three cheers
Hip hip, hip hip, hip hip hooray
We made it together all this way

Now I want you for all eternity
A lifetime seems inadequate you see
I want to be with you forever
My soul won't rest until I endeavour.

The "Benefits" of Age

Sitting alone by the fireside at night
Staring at flames dancing to their delight
A fresh sod of turf renewing their energy
Spiralling the smoke out through the chimney

As the dancers recede to red hot embers
My mind is wandering as it remembers
When this home was once full of laughter
The sound of children reaching the rafter

Only a radio now breaks the silence
To which my sanity is much in reliance
No more do we have end of day reviews
Just silent nights and lonesome blues

So frustrating when minds are still alert
Linked to bodies than can no longer assert
The chores once concluded without hesitation
Are a task now beyond our implementation

To all our children and grandchildren
There is nothing more bewildering
Than to lose one's grip and have no control
When age and illness takes its toll

It's then we need all your loving care
But you may not understand or be aware
Old fogies are reluctant to reach out for aid
We are too stupidly proud, yet so afraid.

The Candlestick Days

Age old fables begin with "In the days of old"
Before electricity came to our fold
When people sat around the open fire
Telling timeworn stories to their hearts desire

Shrewdly placed in a corner was a candlestick
With a candle lazily burning down its wick
Sending its eerie shadows across the room
Feebly attempting to lift the gloom

The kettle was always boiling on the hob
There was a richness without a single bob
You were always welcome to a cup of tae
And the weary traveller was welcomed to stay

Some nights there'd be a fiddle at hand
With a squeeze box and tin whistle you'd have a band
There'd be an all night session of jigs and reels
Singing and dancing and high kicking heels

Brave hearts walking home on the dark lonely lanes
Ghostly sounds curdling the blood in their pulsating veins
Most likely to be a screeching owl on a tree top high
But the banshee's wail was the most fearsome cry

Every little homestead had their own vegetable plot
To be self sufficient meant a lot
There were hens and chickens running around
And the crowing cock was dawn's first sound

The people of this era had a deep faith in the Lord
They would read the bible and listen to the Word
They were at peace with themselves and with God
You might say they were ever ready for the nod.

The Croppy Grave

In the townland of Rathfeigh
Lying in the foothills of Tara so high
A croppy boy lies in his tomb
This is where he met his doom

I have passed this way so very often
You remind me of the longlost and forgotten
When I see your roadside marker
Inscribed 1798, a year none darker

Oh croppy boy we should all weep
Your love for Ireland ran so deep
You marched all the way from Wexford Town
To fight the forces of the crown

Granted you may have held a pike
You didn't deserve to be interred in a dyke
A young man who was so very brave
You deserved to have a proper grave

Did a Padre give you the Last Rite?
And take darkness away and show you light
Or did someone whisper the Act of Contrition
While your soul was parting in another direction

Whenever we are passing through this ward
Let us pause awhile at this little graveyard
To say a prayer for this croppy boy
And hope he has found his peace and joy.

The Mammys Brown Bread

The Mammy's brown bread baked on the griddle
That famous cake crossed in the middle
I've watched her mixing and stirring and kneading
And applying the ingredients without me ever heeding

How I now wish I had that elusive recipe
It was the texture and flavour you see
And the aroma that filled the kitchen
Those fond memories are so bewitching

It was the essence of many's a meal
And many's a hunger pang did it heal
Gilded with some homemade butter
You could only chew and incoherently mutter

You could serve it up with strawberry jam
Or dipped in the grease of the frying pan
You could saturate it with an egg yolk
Habits we inherited from our elder folk

You could talk all day about the Mammy's brown bread
And there still wouldn't be enough said
You could eat it all day and still want more
The Mammy's brown bread is now part of folklore

Nowadays there are cereal and breakfast bars
People are consuming as they drive their cars
Eating their breakfast as to work they sped
Not like sitting down to the Mammy's brown bread

So many memories of the Mammy's brown bread
Her skill with the grill and how I was fed
Growing up in the fiftys and sixtys was tough
But her brown bread provided me enough.

The Proper Antidote

With no one to talk to and feeling alone
And the weight of the world on my shoulder bone
When nothing I do seems to go right
And I feel like giving up the good fight
When there doesn't seem to be any way out
Reason becomes silent and insanity will shout
Some of you will think my antidote risky
But my medication is a bottle of Whiskey.

The Road to No Return

We spray our crops and kill our bees
Doing untold damage no one sees
Harming the wildlife we adorn
Are we on the road to no return?

Fouling our rivers polluting our seas
Contaminating the air that will cause us to wheeze
Viewing our scientists with baneful scorn
Are we on the road to no return?

Artificial chemicals and insecticides
Antidepressants and suicides
Living a life of such forlorn
Are we on the road to no return?

Opportunists jumping on bandwagons
In pursuit of free rides and shaggings
Never thinking to adjourn
Are we on the road to no return?

Extracting coal and oil from Earths bowels
To pollute the skies through chimney cowls
No one raising a voice of concern
Are we on the road to no return?

Mother Nature is warning us all
Our orb will become a raging fireball
The world we know will scorch and burn
Are we on the road to no return?

Through Purple Haze

(To the Class of 61)

Comrades from my past, how are you all
It gives me great pleasure, to make this call
Not to be with you in person is with regret
But this is a moment I'll cherish and never forget

I can't leave my wife in her time of need
My forgiveness from you I plead
My love and care for her exceeds all
Remorse would overcome me, not being on call

Still, technology offers us this virtual meeting
It's not perfection but still a greeting
Seems I'm destined never to shake your hand
Fate is difficult to grasp, or understand

Life was harsh to some of our comrades
A sombre reminder of six short decades
When we first crossed the Brosna River
Filled with anticipation and frenzied quiver

There were names I confess, I had forgotten
But for the pen of Jim Harkin and his jotting
Thank you Jim, for bringing me this close
To all still living, and those in repose

You rescued me from my amnestic lapse,
Bridging the memories through vacant gaps.
I'll remember you all for the rest of my days
As I gaze back to sixty one, through purple haze.

To Have a Magic Wand

If only I had a magic wand
To wave and spread happiness far beyond
I'd rid the world of every evil
And placate all life of upheaval

If only I had a magic wand
And give to everyone what they're fond
To see only smiling faces
Even in the most dour of places

If only I had a magic wand
And right all for those who were wronged
That they be able to pick up the pieces
Before all quality time ceases

If only I had a magic wand
I would compose a special bond
Between archenemies and stringent foe
And illuminate their world aglow

If only I had a magic wand
And bestow upon those who have longed
For true love and romance
So what, if it is the last dance

If only I had a magic wand
I would create a most heavenly pond
Filled with fishes for the kingfisher blue
And a swan with her cygnets swimming in queue.

Trade Not Time for Dreams

It's astonishing how quick we age
Every day is just another page
To a story we don't record
Except for memories we dare to hoard

All that time spent on worry
Racing, scurrying, always in a hurry
Running around from here to there
With little progress and getting nowhere

Slow down, don't chase the pace
Stay clear of the rat infested race
Keep life simple and uncomplicated
Get rich schemes tend to be ill-fated

Don't anchor yourself down with debt
So many have, and wept
Ruthless lenders seek their bounty
Sheriffs lurking in every county

Live life prudent and within your means
Enjoy the rainbows and panoramic scenes
God gave us a world full of pleasure
For all to enjoy at our leisure

Stress and burden speeds up time
Denies you freedom when in your prime
One day you'll realise you are now old
Whilst chasing dreams your time you sold.

We Too Were Once Oppressed

There's resentment lurking in our land
And hatred's flames are being fanned
Emerging upon a dispirited refugee
Who from his war-torn land, had to flee

Lessons from our bloody history seem lost
When our forefathers fled the holocaust
The hungry millions who stayed and died
For years our people mourned and cried

Blame not the refugee for being one
But the warmongers who caused him to flee and run
May we welcome the tortured and distressed
For we ourselves were once oppressed

Government policies have created divisions
Neglecting our own of essential provisions
Instigating acrimony and discontentment
Arousing anger and resentment

We must never forsake our own
And all those children without a home
The lost souls living rough on the street
With no shelter or place to retreat

Let us all stand united and steadfast
Never forgetting our horrendous past
Not to wish the same upon others
Soften our hearts and live as sisters and brothers.

What's the Harm

What's the harm in having a night cap
When caught up in the old age trap
What harm will a skinful do
If it feels like it's overdue
When too old to become violent
And hoarse enough to remain silent
If your lips are too chapped to be kissed
Sure what's the harm in getting pissed.

Who is Your Mum?

Your mum is that person you will miss most

When she's gone and no longer your host

Your mum is that person that always cared for you

When she's gone there will be times you'll rue

Your mum is that person that always worried

When she's gone all greatness is buried

Your mum is that person if you still have her

Love her as you should and always be there

Happy Mother's Day!

With Best Intentions

I lived my life the best I could
Though not always as it should
I blasphemed and cursed and swore
As it if were a daily chore

I lived my life the best I could
Searching for ways to do some good
Causing no hurt to my fellow man
For political correctness I was never a fan

I lived my life the best I could
Perspiring and toiling in muck and mud
Bent and stooped with an aching back
Seeking relief from the local quack

I lived my life the best I could
Alternating from ice cold veins to heated blood
Cold and calm or temper flared
Sometimes brave and often scared

I lived my life the best I could
I saw the life of spring begin to bud
I watched the seasons come and go
And sheltered from the winters snow

I lived my life the best I could
And gazed at the stars from where I stood
I bowed my head in silent prayer
Knowing Heaven is someplace up there

You Didn't Hear Me

You didn't hear me come to bed
I stayed up awhile instead
Waiting for you to go asleep
A peaceful slumber, till mornings keep

You didn't hear me come to bed
My pillow wouldn't rest my head
Until I knew you were at ease
And hear you snore as you please

You didn't hear me come to bed
In the silence a tear I shed
Knowing you've done no evil
So undeserving of this upheaval

You didn't hear me come to bed
For softly on the floor I thread
To see you rest free from pain
Shows me my faith is not in vain

You didn't hear me come to bed
Sweet dreams were in your head
Your calm and composed expression
Told me there was no aggression

You didn't hear me come to bed
I waited up until my prayers I said
To our guardian angel for safekeeping
During the night whilst we are sleeping

You Never Forget to Pray

I watched you gaze into the empty space
And I saw the anguish on your grimaced face
A face that once beamed the sweetest smile
Rivalled only by your elegant style

This relentless suffering and affliction
Is contributing daily to your restriction
Limbs that once danced all through the night
Are no longer capable of standing upright

Your independence is so compromised
And your life's rituals all revised
Every little thing that mattered
Is ravaged and wholly shattered

I beg a cure will come your way
And rid you of this illness of decay
I dream of us living our autumn years
With good health, that would allay our fears

But tears fill my ageing eyes
When I hear your distressing cries
Anger and frustration comes over me
When I'm unable to execute your plea

Yet, you never forget to pray
Each night and every day
A miracle, you truly deserve
For all your hope and unending verve

A Monumental Bender

Drinking whiskey and beer is a great pastime
We drink ourselves stupid until we can't even mime
Lowering it down and putting on a silly pout
A contorted face with not a sound coming out
But the last thing I'd do is to surrender
When I'm out on a monumental bender

We planned a night out with a few lads
Some were drinkers and some only tads
It started off quietly, just a few sober pints
Too slow for some so they started smoking joints
And some not happy till they met the opposite gender
On the night of a monumental bender

The music and craic soon got going
Some didn't know what they were doing
The craic was great until a pint got knocked
And all of a sudden someone got clocked
All hell broke loose as far as I can remember
On the night of a monumental bender

Law and order was at last restored
But not before a few got floored
Pandemonium was soon brought to an end
The hurt and injured we had to tend
Bandages and plasters we had to render
It was on the night of a monumental bender

Some time the next day when I woke up
With distant memories of a night of disrupt
Lifting my head from my soft cosy pillow
Suddenly I felt like a weeping willow
Thinking where would I find the nearest whiskey vendor
On the morning after a monumental bender

So here is to my new found sobriety
No more drinking whiskey for me
Famous last words after the night before
But recovery comes and that's for sure
Drinking again like a full time contender
For the next bloody monumental bender.

A Smiling Face A Crying Heart

I feel so helpless watching your decline
My face may smile but my heart is crying
I don't want you to see my pain
For yours is more than I could ever retain

I have often asked my God, why?
Good people like you get little joy
I get no answers, I receive no replies
My quests go unanswered, I'm no more wise

All I wanted was our good health
But without yours I have no wealth
Friends, worldly possessions mean nothing
When your loved one is in pain and hurting

I wouldn't wish this on my worst enemy
And I'd pray their garden is not Gethsemane
I just wish mine was the Garden of Eden
Where the forbidden apple we could still be eating.

A Visit In Peace

The old country churchyard glistening with frost
Tis early morn with darkness just lost,
The deafening silence is the only sound,
And the crunch of feet on the snow white ground.

The sun is rising over yonder in the East,
Casting shadows over this place of peace,
It's a good time to visit these Holy Grounds,
No interruptions only natural sounds.

The old church ruin still has its bell
It's awhile now since we heard it's last knell
High up on the gable facing the West
Like our beloved deceased, it's left to rest

The daffodils are out in full bloom
They help erase some of the gloom
Their golden heads dancing in the breeze
Caressing your soul and setting you at ease

Walking around you will take note of a name
Some of notoriety and some of great fame
Now that they are all children of God
There'll be no more villainy from under the sod

My last call is to my Mother and Father
The flowers in the vases are needing water
I'll say my few words and be on my way
It's a great comfort to be able to pray.

Convulsive Verse by an Ordinary Person

Speak not again Israel of the holocaust
The sympathy of this world you have lost
You became more cruel than your aggressor
You learned well to become the oppressor

The world is mourning for the little kids
You murdered in their hospital beds
The indiscriminate bombing by your sonic jets
Causing bloody maiming and promiscuous deaths

Never again claim to be the chosen ones of God
You are the devil's disciple on this land you trod
What righteous God would stand by and condone
Your shameful sins, what kind of God would atone?

Benjamin Netanyahu you have questions to answer
Your Mossad police force are a cancer
Their propaganda is steeped with lies
Thankfully the people are now more wise

The utterances from their propagandist mouths
Come faster than swear words from street louts
Spewing falsities and untruths
Astonishingly there are governments still in cahoots

I pray to The One who once walked this land
At a time of heathenism, and the Romans manned
That He'll decide it's time to return again
And rid these children of their sorrow and pain.

Cursed Emigration

Emigration is the scourge of our race,
Every few years it's what parents face,
We rear our children the best we can,
We're just preparing them for a foreign land

The pain and heartache families endure,
Our heartless leaders leave us insecure,
No wonder there's apathy among our youth,
When it comes to elections they don't give a hoot

We bring them to ports with a one way fare,
The ruling classes haven't a care,
The hugs and kisses and the sad goodbyes,
Grandparents watching with watery eyes

Grandparents lives can be as dark as night,
They have two families in this awful plight,
Looking at their child waving goodbye to their children,
In their Autumn years, it is very bewildering

There are no leaders to inspire,
Only power will fulfil their desire,
Our heroes of The Rising would be aggrieved,
To see what followed, obsessed with greed

Our corrupt system has to change,
And give our young a decent wage,
God and country they could serve,
It's the very least that they deserve.

Don't Ask Me To Do The Dishes

My cooking skills are not so bad
To rustle up some grub I'd be only glad
I'd toss together something delicious
Just don't ask me to do the dishes

I can boil a pot of scalding water
And make you a cuppa to order
I'll read the tealeaves to fulfil your wishes
Just don't ask me to do the dishes

An expert at cooking a hardboiled egg
If you don't believe me, to differ I'll beg
Guess you're now laughing, maybe in stitches
Just don't ask me to do the dishes

If you ask me for a slice of toast
'Tis the best I will surely boast
To get a serving you'd have to be precious
Just don't ask me to do the dishes

My culinary skills are of plenty
Sure your belly would never be empty
Your appetite gratified with savoury riches
Just don't ask me to do the dishes

I surely am not telling you lies
Or ingesting you with porky pies
No need for you to be suspicious
Just don't ask me to do the dishes.

Echoes From Long Ago

Our changing wildlife we should fear,
The loss of sounds we use to hear,
The sounds from our childhood long ago,
Sounds that our children don't even know

Man has improved his humble life,
In his progress he is causing strife,
Oh Mother Earth you should give us warning,
About all the habitat we are harming

All those that have disappeared,
No longer to be seen or heard,
This is a loss we will not regain,
This is a loss and a terrible pain

To hear the corncrake, his croaky voice,
We have lost this sound not by choice,
Progress by stealth we've lost a lot,
All these pleasures forget us not

The sound of the cuckoo in purple haze,
In wonder and awe I would gaze,
Living in hope to get a glimpse,
Of that wee bird our summer prince

So I ask you God if you can,
Have a word with my fellow man,
Or wake him up from his stupid slumber,
And save our habitat from a lesser number.

Ninety Seconds to Midnight

Our hallowed world is in a perilous place
Dire consequences awaits the human race
Mankind is on course to self destruction
Levers and buttons primed for atomic eruption

Nothing to gain and to lose so much
An agitated mind or accidental touch
And it's back to the planet of the apes
Contorted bodies in all kinds of shapes

A nuclear war will bring cataclysmic drought
Look what Hiroshima, Nagasaki and Chernobyl brought
Our world will become desolate and famished
And all our species diminished or vanished

Greed and power is all it takes
For a despot to up the stakes
Words of provocation, mockery and scorn
And the will for dialogue will then be spurn

To those seeking notoriety, fame will be naught
No witnesses to who fired the first shot
With complete obliteration of mankind's existence
A world left in darkness and eerie silence

Were we humans here before I often query
It's not beyond credence, my eccentric theory
Were we more advanced than we are now
Did man before look up at the plough

So many unexplained mysteries from our past
The construction of the pyramids, gigantic and vast
The accuracy of New Grange on winter's solstice
The analyses from scientists are just not suffice.

Our Destiny

We do our best to cope together
Though at times its heavy weather
Without hesitation we both agree
It seems uncertain, our destiny

Together we do the best we can
You're still my girl and I'm your man
Not far ahead can we see
It seems uncertain, our destiny

We walked side by side on this long road
With our children we shared a happy abode
Now all flown from the nest it's just you and me
It seems uncertain, our destiny

My heart is yours if it's any use
If not I can make no excuse
I have done all I could you see
It seems uncertain, our destiny

One thing is sure if not certain
From this I will not dishearten
I'll take care of you with the greatest glee
It seems uncertain, our destiny

It breaks my heart to see your pain
From dark clouds there pours teeming rain
There's no shelter from the foliaged tree
It seems uncertain, our destiny

I do ask our God to be kind
To at least give us peace of mind
To forgive us and bestow his clemency
And together we'll reach our final destiny.

Samuel They Can Kiss My Ass

I hear your whisper Old Samuel as I pour
You are bringing up conversations we had before
The unlikely friendship we struck up
Fate you say, I say it was luck

Without a virus we might never have met
I admit you rescued my sanity when I began to fret
With nowhere to go and nothing to do
You appeared from nowhere out of the blue

Whenever now there's a time of crises
And experts chin-wagging their ill gotten advices
Me and you just arrange a get-together
Come what storms we will weather

Life is too short for unnecessary worry
We sort out our problems in an expedient hurry
Our wicked sense of humour few will condone
But together we will never be alone

Every time I unscrew the cork
Of the bottle in which you lurk
Is like letting the genie go free
Without three wishes just a drinking spree

Forever grateful Old Samuel and I therefore pledge
No soul between us will drive a wedge
When I tilt and pour you into my glass
The whole world can go and kiss my ass.

Simply For Tish

Patricia Loughran since you became my wife,
You changed my world, you changed my life,
If I hadn't met you where would I be,
More than likely I'd be all at sea

Your enchanting smile anchored me to Earth,
A son and two daughters in healthy birth,
You done it all in your own little stride,
All I could do was to be at your side

To be at your side I am very proud,
I want to shout and tell the world out loud,
Without your genteel and simple way,
My whole life would be in total disarray

So here is to us Patricia, or Tish,
This would be my very last wish,
We'd walk into our sunset holding hands,
And we'd start all over in The Forever Lands.

Splendid Conditions

A silvery moon is high in the sky,
In the faraway distance, a banshee's cry.
An eeriness lies across the mountainy hill
As the embers burn beneath the still.
The potatoes and barley are in the pot,
And the excise man asleep in his cot.
Conditions are splendid for poteen distilling,
In moonshine, we'll soon all be a swilling.

Spring

You can see the stretch in the evenings now
Soon time for winter to take a bow
Nature is readying to re-awaken
And renew the life it had forsaken

Our star is returning to our hemisphere
And our songbirds we'll soon again hear
Greeting the dawn with vigour and verve
A cuisine of sound they adroitly serve

Spring bulbs are bursting through the clay
Anxious to give us their floral display
Feverishly exploding into bloom
Eradicating the forlorn winter gloom

Spring in the air puts a spring in our step
A tonic more uplifting than pills for our pep
Reinvigorating life into body and soul
Rejuvenating our ambition and goal

There's a smell of freshness in the air
It's the newness of another year
There are unique challenges to be faced
Especially if you are feeling outpaced

But we are still ahead of the hibernator
Who is still dreaming of sometime later
Giving us mortals that little head start
Of those wee critters that work so hard

Don't you all feel it in your bones
This time of year gives more vibrant tones
It has so much umph, get up and go
There's a new seasons seed to sow.

The Howling Winds

Looking out my window at the night sky
A speeding moon seems to float by
An illusionary vision created by a rolling cloud
The celestial light dimmed by its shroud

The tree tops appear to stoop and bow
Genuflecting and making a vow
Blow wind blow for tonight you will not lower
When you're out of breath I still shall tower

I'm here writing in the candlelight
With a glowing fire and embers bright
It's cosy listening to the howling winds
I pray for the safety of all my friends

These storms are now given names
Some are male the rest are dames
For whatever reason I do not know
But male or female they sure can blow

They now forecast tornadoes and twisters
Certainly none of them come in whispers
Will o'the wisp was once a sensation
Wondering now was it a dwarf relation

The time was we recognised all seasons
Accepting their weather without any grievance
We knew the time to sow and reap
Hibernators knew when to waken and sleep.

Two Hearts Of Gold

(Tribute to Jimmy and Ciss)

Jimmy and Ciss, I'm so in debt
Your hospitality I'll not forget
You accepted me into your fold
Two precious hearts of gold

Never hesitant nor did you pause
To react generously to a needy cause
Your strategy always swift and bold
Two precious hearts of gold

We had good times together
The four of us in tether
Better to leave some tales untold
Two precious hearts of gold

You're an inspiration to us all
Gave us the courage to stand up tall
You showed us how to grow gracefully old
Two precious hearts of gold.

What They Call Graceful

Growing old and getting grumpy
Your porridge making has become more lumpy
The soft boiled eggs are getting harder
Because your rambling mind is wandering farther

You're wearing braces in lieu of a belt
Seems your waist has expanded by stealth
Not now able to stand on one leg
To put a sock on the other peg

Bending down to tie a lace
No longer can be done in haste
Everything is performed in slower motion
With extreme care and added caution

When the battery dies in your hearing aid
Every sound seems like a serenade
Soft and low and beautifully mellow
As soothing as the acoustics of a cello

When the hair disappears from your head
And there's a shine up there instead
When there's no more use for brush or comb
Sit back and admire your elegant dome

Shaving now spells trouble
For the face and not the stubble
The nicks and cuts and abrasions
Followed by foul mouthed orations

Alas, when you see your teeth in a glass
That smiling tumbler looks crass
To see the sight of them every morning
Is enough to kill a yawning.

Whittling Away The Hours

I want to take this opportunity
And can I say it with impunity
You must all be stone mad
To indulge in words from my pad

Yet I have to say I do appreciate
Your kind comments and how you rate
To each poem I put on display
Never do you cause me any dismay

The reason I sit down to write
Is to whittle away the hours at night
A pastime to which I'm now addicted
And a taste for bourbon I've become afflicted

Critics there are I have no doubt
Their opinions they do not flout
I'm aware of their need to cringe and weep
I hail the silence they politely keep

Poetry is not a cure-all for everyone
It can be drab and tedious to the bone
Uninteresting and unflattering to the core
Stodgy and stuffy and a downright bore

But to all you resolute followers
Words are not for feckless borrowers
Just one remark misspent
Might cause a lifetime of repent.

Who Can Say

Who can say for certain
We done enough on the Earth and
Expect to pass through the pearly gates
Where angels in eternal Heaven awaits

Who can say without any doubt
We know what we're doing and what we're about
That we'll cross that great divide
And be seated on the right hand side

Who can say for sure
Their body and soul is cleansed and pure
As they breathe their very last breath
The moment before their death

Who can say I'm sincerely sorry
So contrite they'll have no worry
Knowing they have truly repented
And God's anger will not be vented

Who can say with positivity
They truly accept the nativity
That the Son of God came upon this Earth
A stable was His place of birth

Who can say with conviction
They believe in the crucifixion
The crowning with the thorns
In Jesus death, the world mourns

Who can say for sure
They won't have to endure
The loss of God's love for all eternity
Who can say with certainty.

Who Cares

Who cares about inebriation or sobriety
We humans are a diversified variety
Some look down their elongated noses
Others think their excrement smell of roses

Who cares about stiff upper lips
Or them drinking hot toddies in sips
And those with a vocabulary so grandiose
Sure that all changes when the liquor flows

Who cares about posers in pinstripe suits
Or those who wear wellington boots
They all came into this world stark naked
And they'll leave it a lot less sacred

Who cares about million or billionaires
They worry not about those sleeping in thoroughfares
Their mansions down long tree lined avenues
Are as vain as their lives and garden pews

Who cares about what we take to drink
But alcohol may alter the way we think
Plans usually peak when we get drunk
The morning after they are all sunk

God gave us alcohol as a great leveller
To bring equality to all class of reveller
The stupid begin to think they know it all
While the astute reasoning starts to stall.

ABOUT THE AUTHOR

Desmond Lynch was born in the beautiful County Meath, Ireland, in a quaint little village called Ardcath. He is married and has three grown-up children and many grandchildren. Desmond discovered his love for writing after he left work to become a full-time carer for his beloved wife, Tish.

Printed in Great Britain
by Amazon

e94ee5d7-7c4a-480d-a9c7-0c365f0d9b16R01